Poorman Doodles

Artwork by Master Doodle Artist

Kevin Poorman

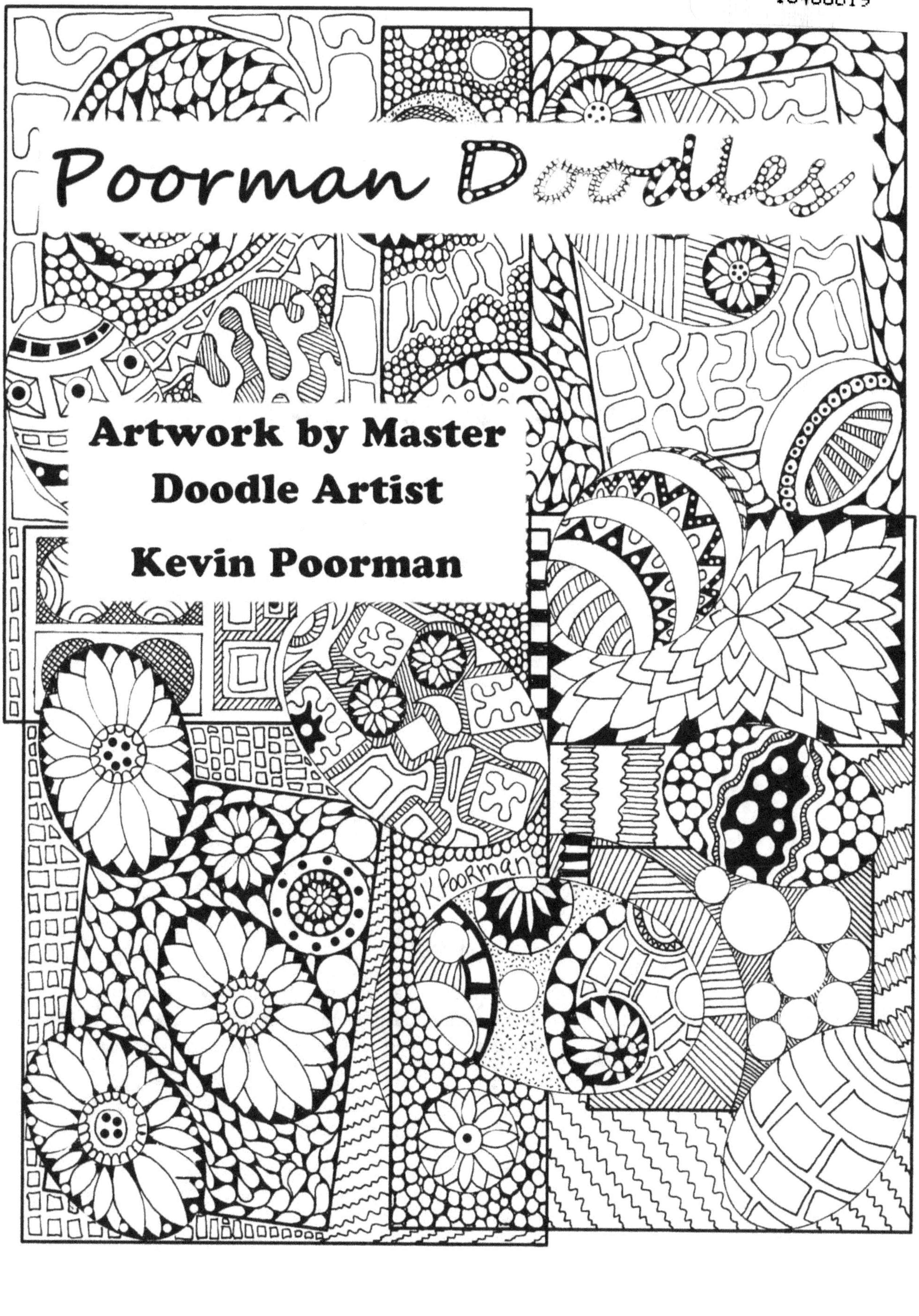

Poorman Doodles

Positive Themes

About the Artist

Kevin Poorman is an artist, photographer and puzzle-maker living in Lorton, Virginia. He grew up in Southern Indiana where his family owned and operated an artist supplies and picture framing business catering to area artists and art students attending Vincennes University.

Kevin's preferred art medium is pen and black ink. This book contains 20 of Kevin's most recent pen and ink drawings, many with floral themes. Enjoy hours of coloring the varied intricate patterns and challenging designs.

In the last few years, Kevin ventured into making jigsaw puzzles from his artwork and photographs. His puzzles are available at several historical venues in Northern Virginia, including George Mason's plantation at Gunston Hall, the Manassas National Battlefield, the Fairfax City Museum, as well as various gift and specialty shops, including Puzzle Palooza, Etc., in Occoquan, and T & K Treasures Specialty Gifts in Clifton, Virginia.

Please see the full line of Kevin's drawings, photographs and puzzles at www.puzzlecuts.com .

Email comments to: puzzlecuts@gmail.com

Enjoy coloring!

Contents

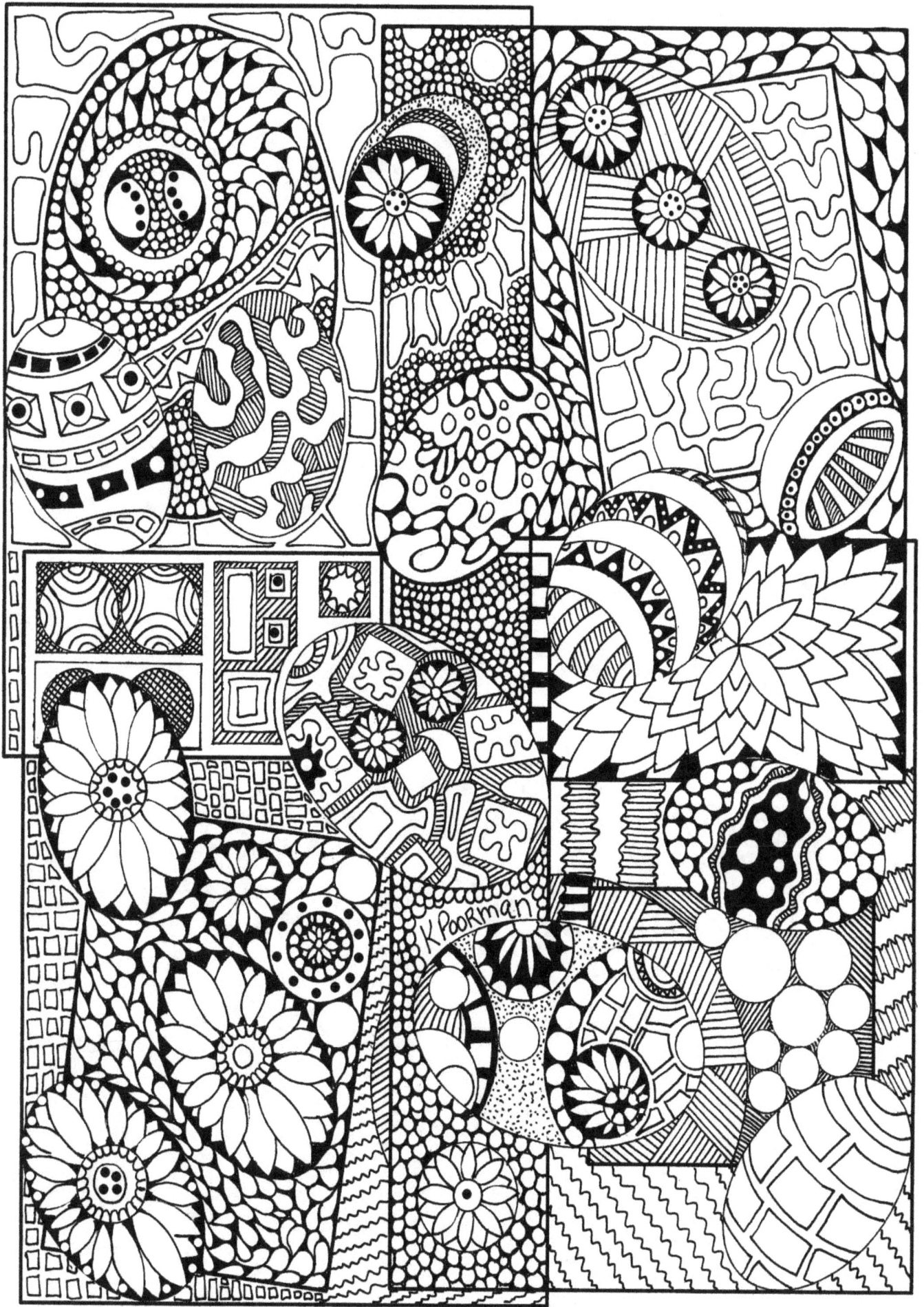

This blank page serves as a blotter
page to absorb marker ink that
might bleed through while coloring.

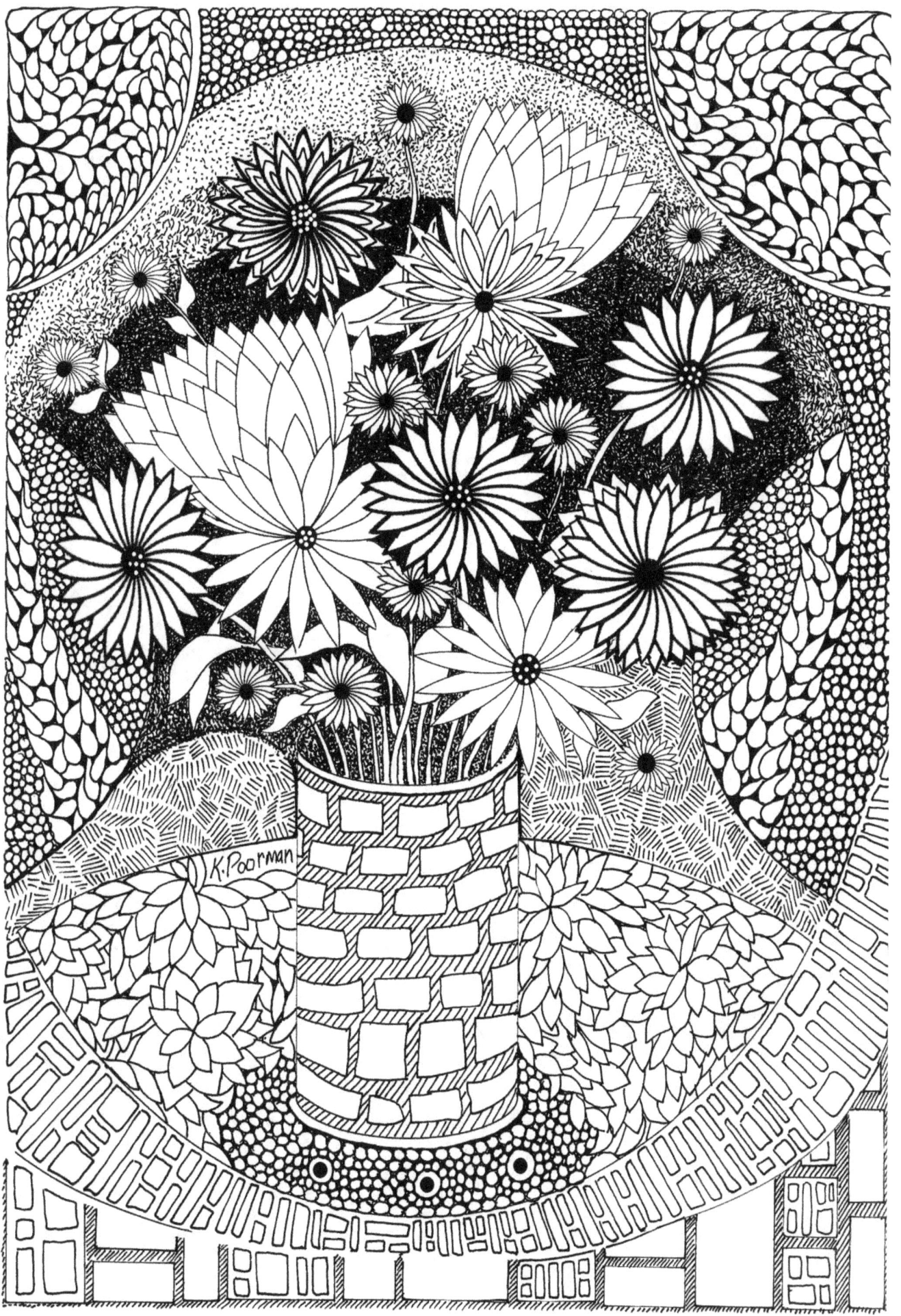

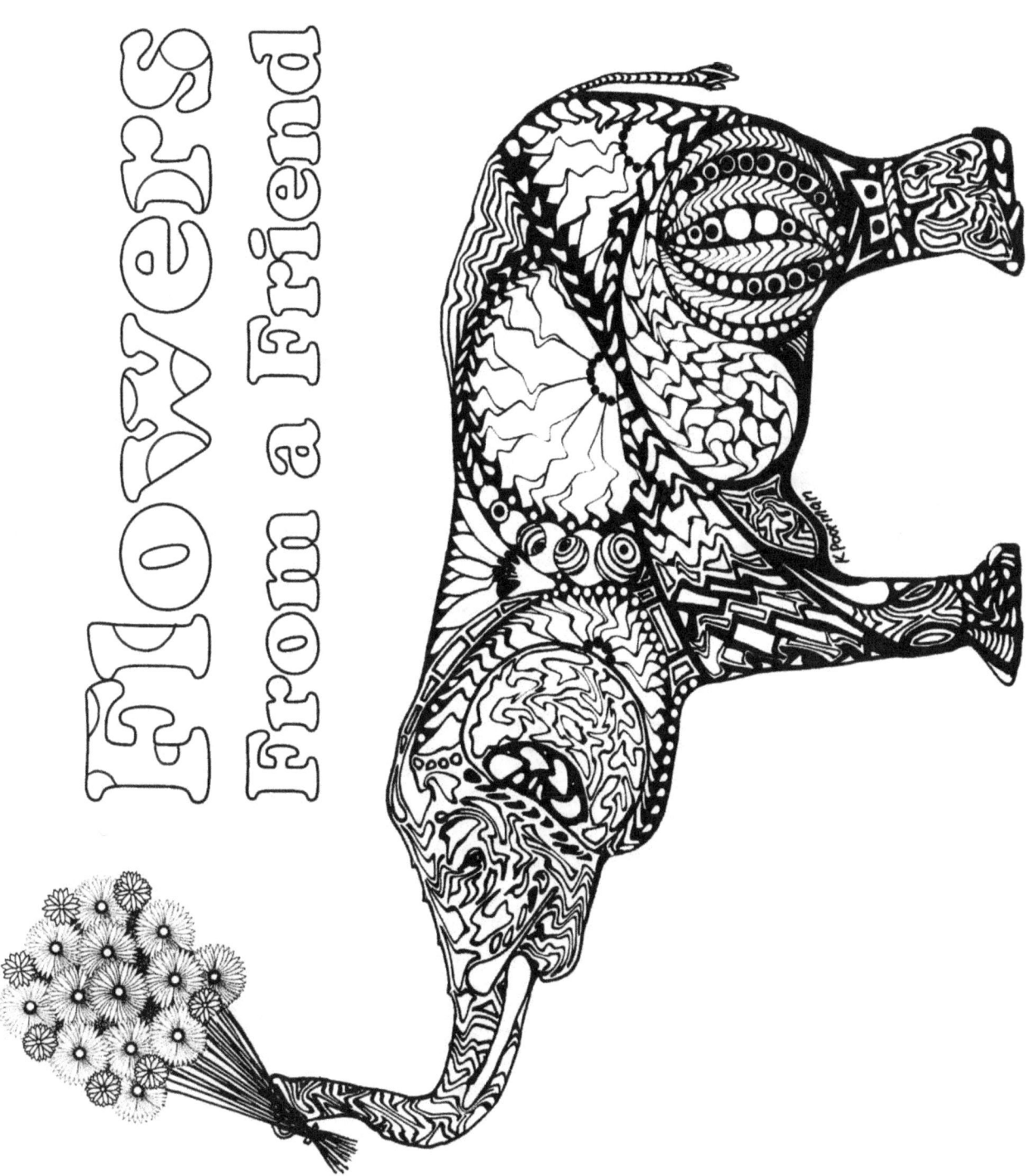

Flowers
From a Friend

This blank page serves as a blotter page to absorb marker ink that might bleed through while coloring.

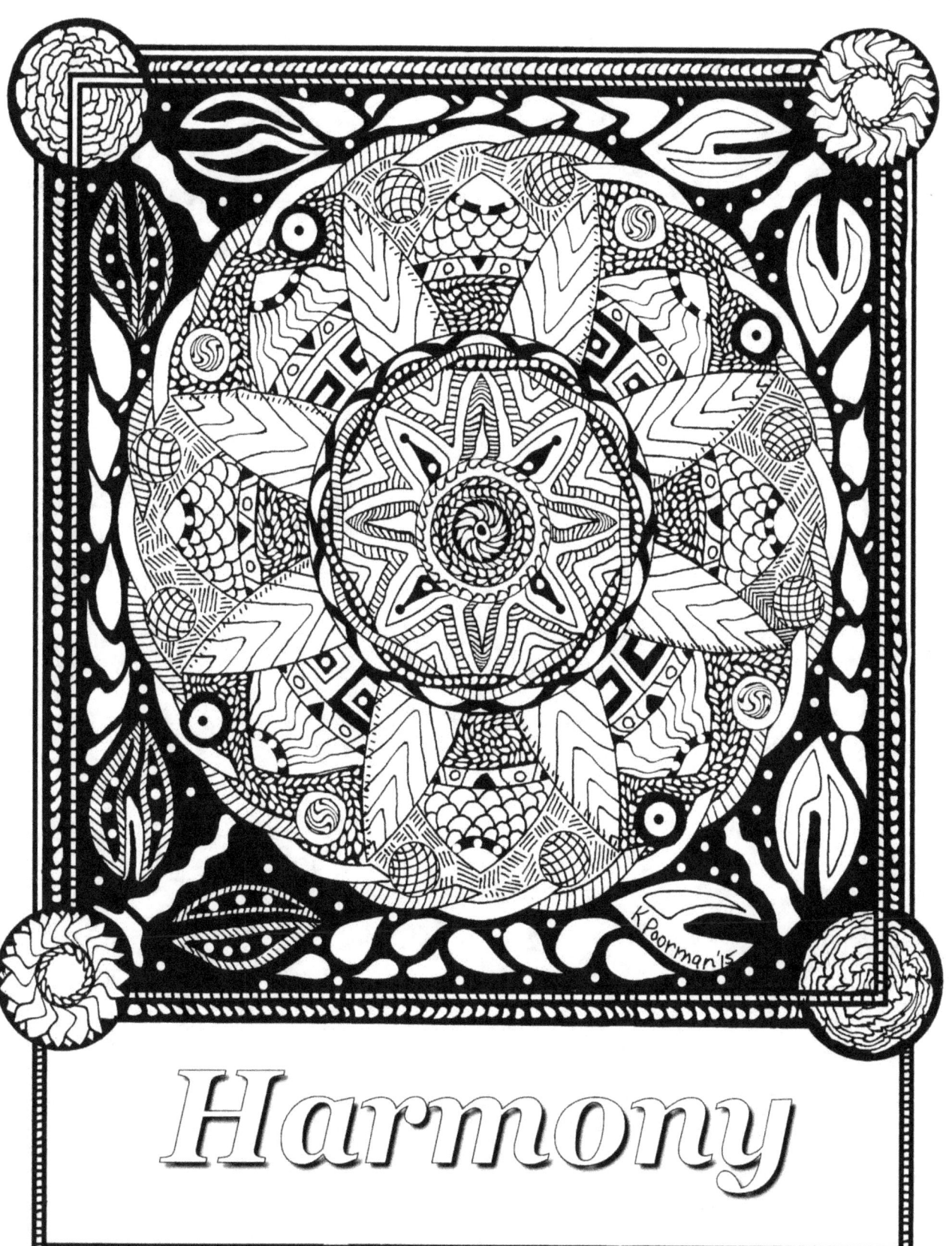

Harmony

This blank page serves as a blotter page to absorb marker ink that might bleed through while coloring.

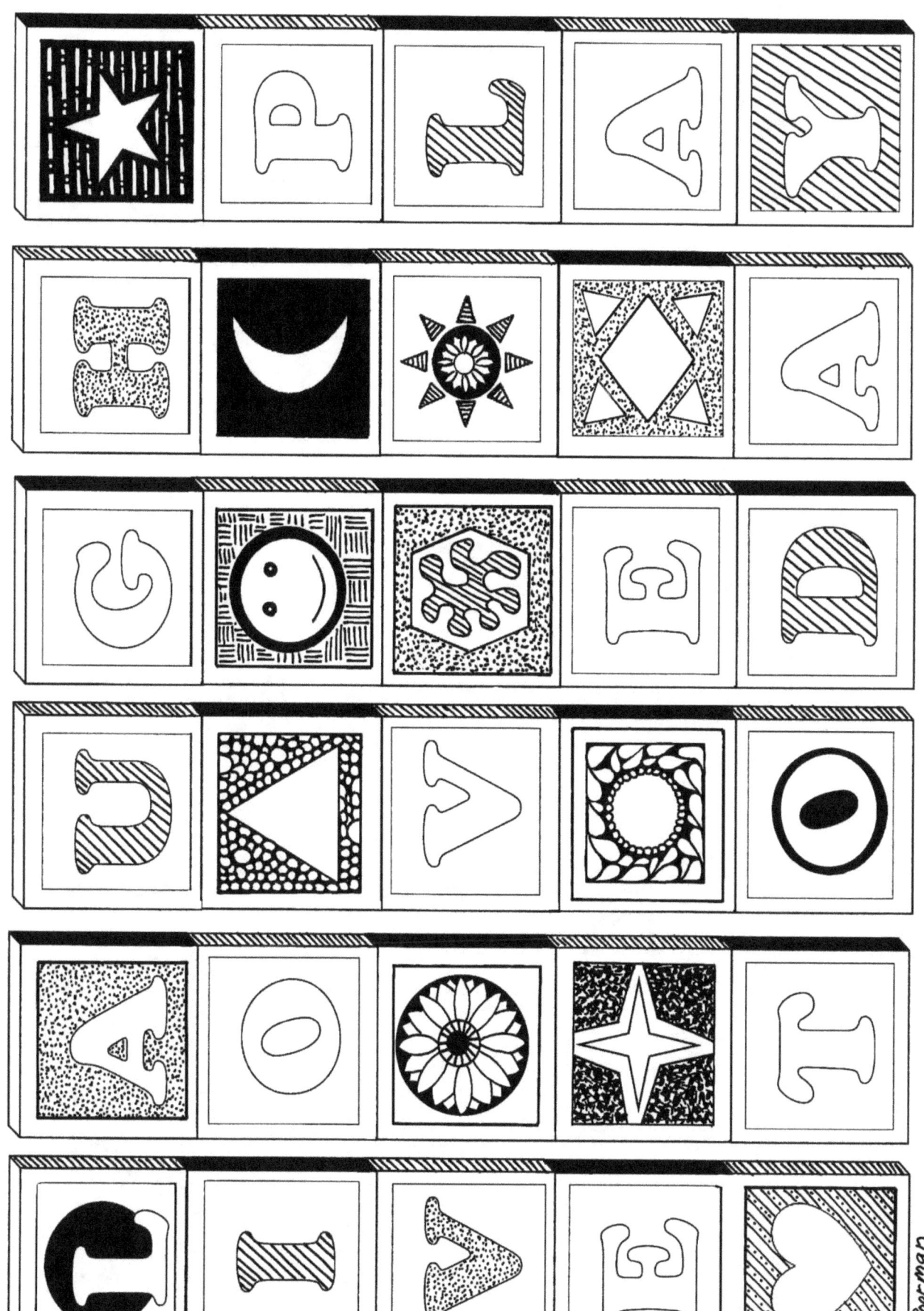

This blank page serves as a
blotter page to absorb marker
ink that might bleed through
while coloring.

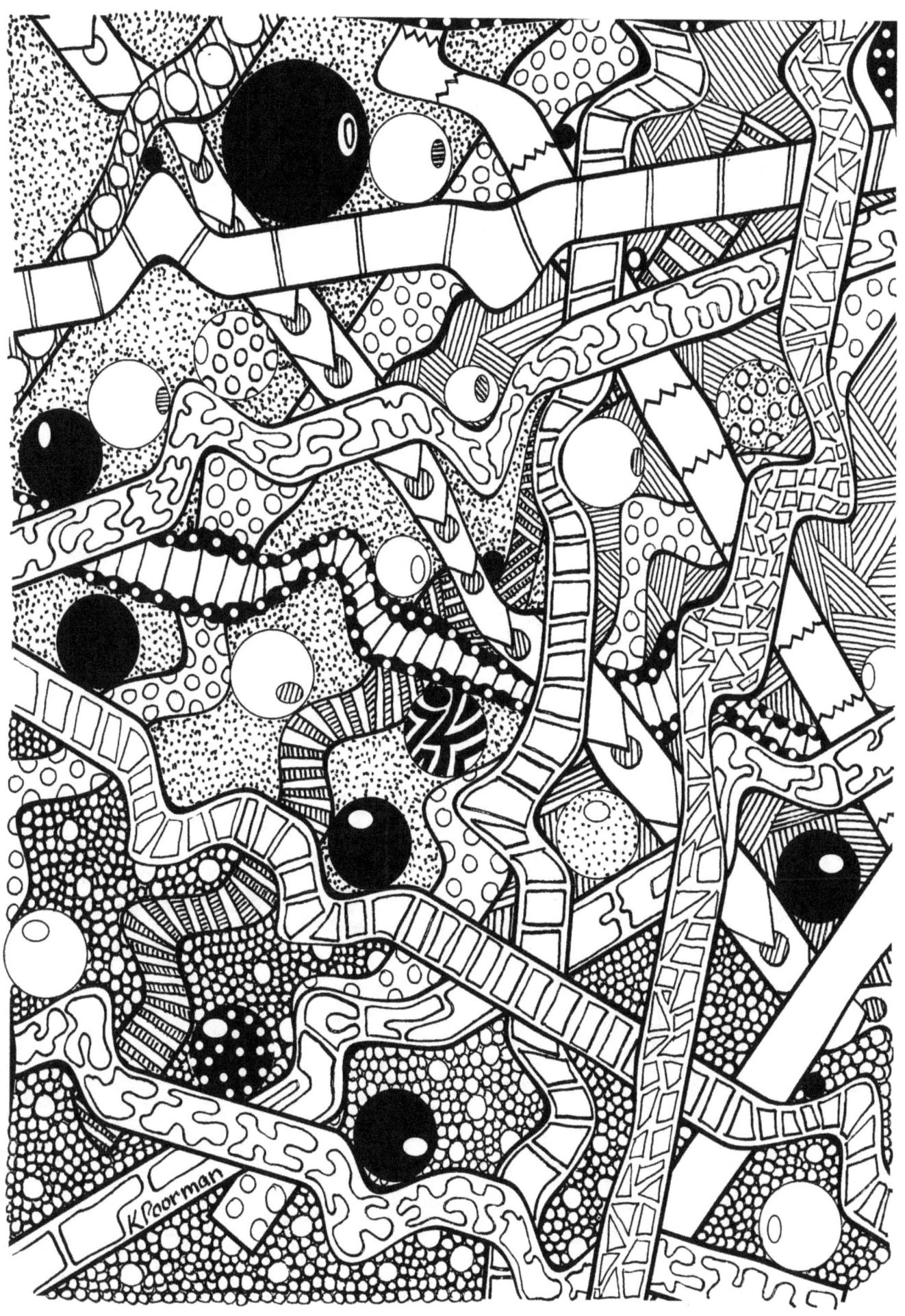

This blank page serves as a blotter page to absorb marker ink that might bleed through while coloring.

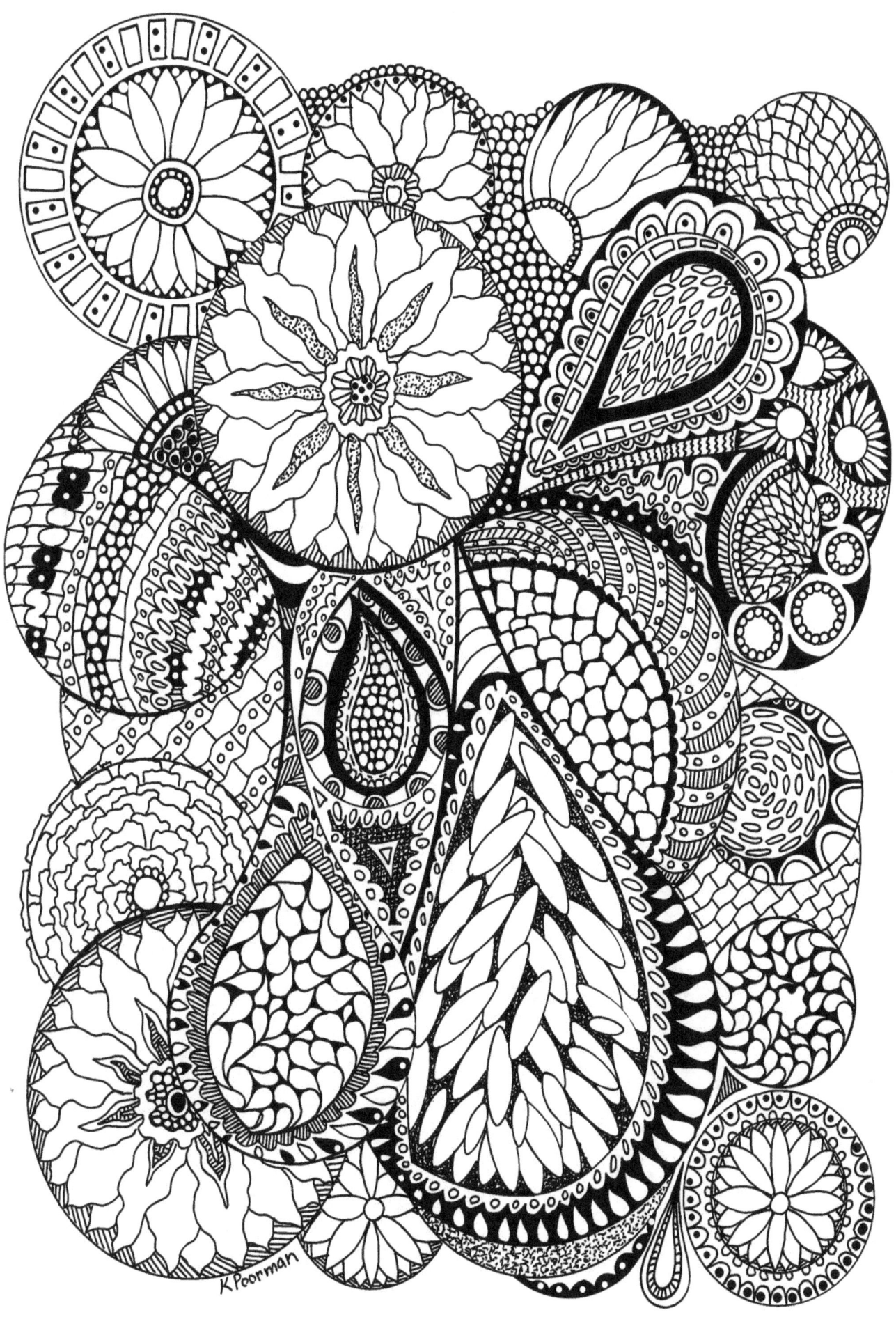
K Poorman

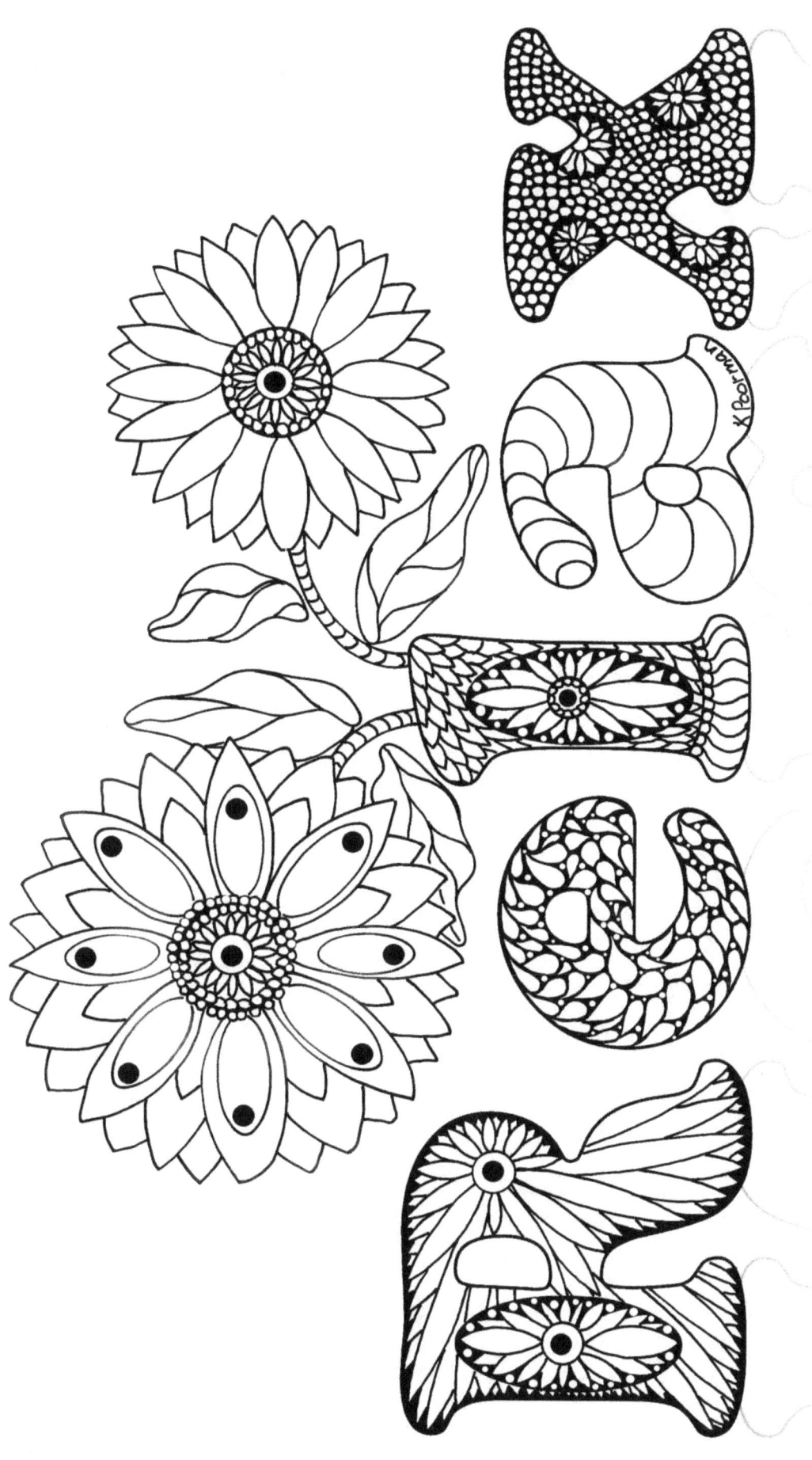

This blank page serves as a blotter page to absorb marker ink that might bleed through while coloring.

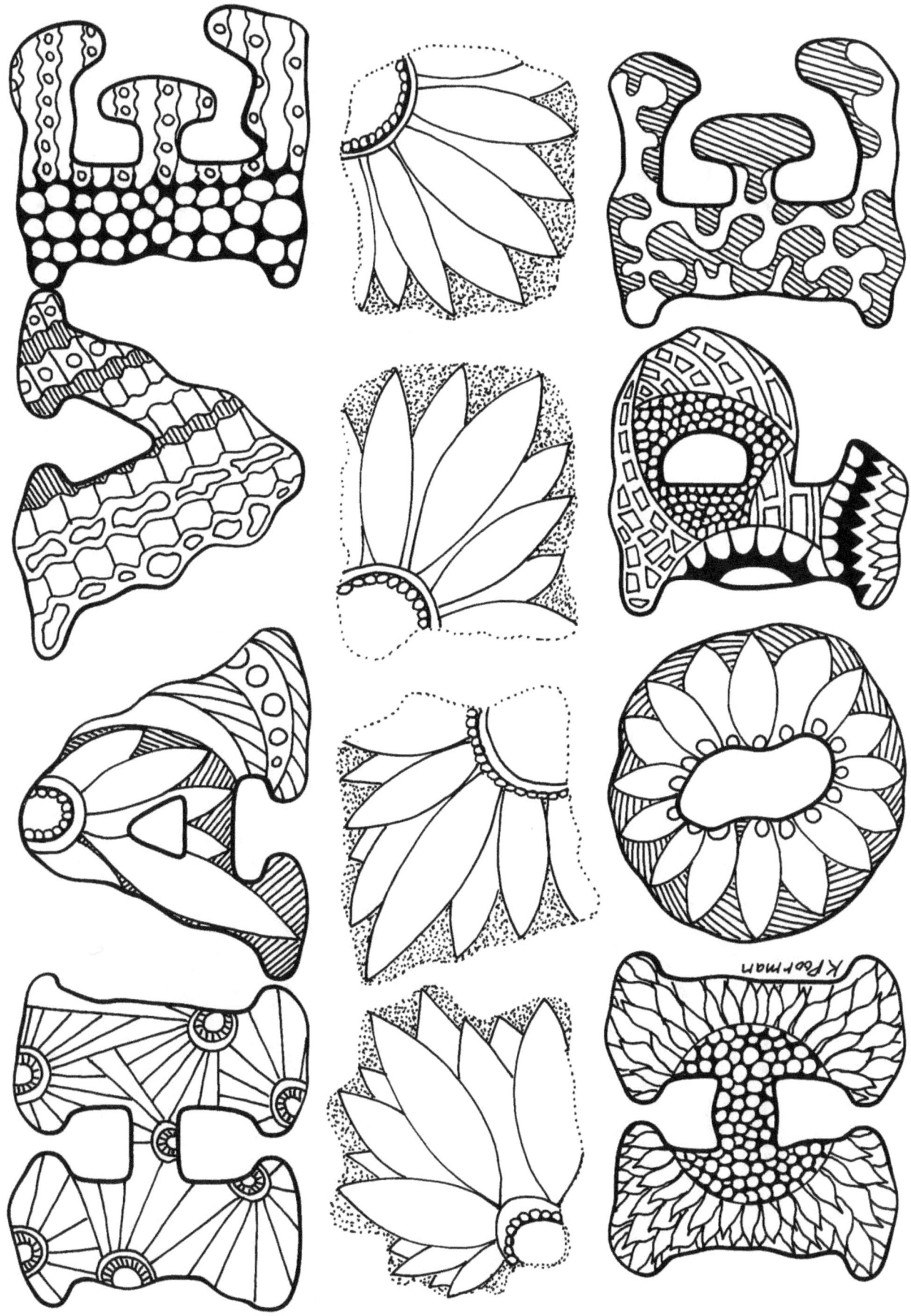

This blank page serves as a blotter page to absorb marker ink that might bleed through while coloring.

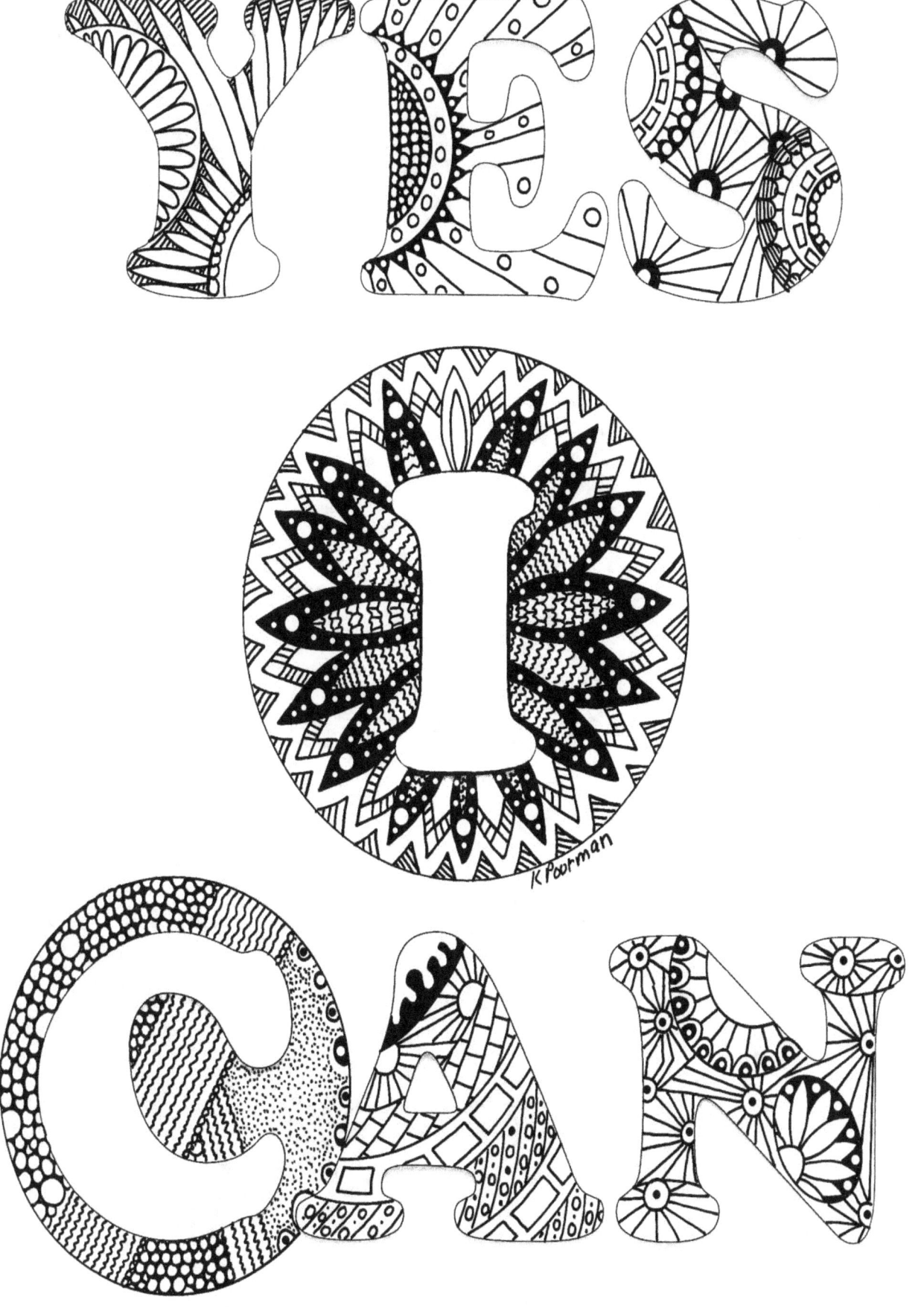

This blank page serves as a
blotter page to absorb marker
ink that might bleed through
while coloring.

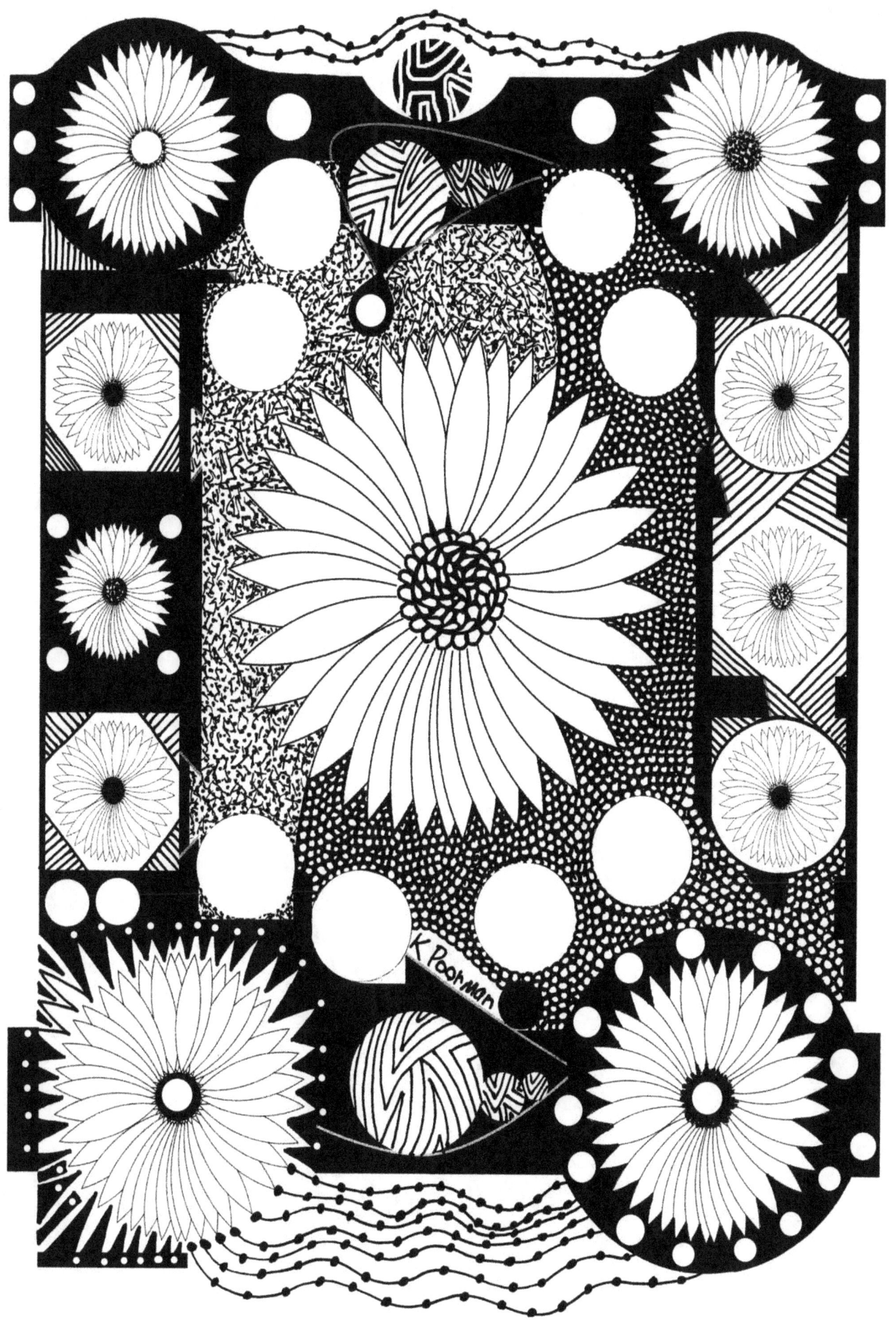

This blank page serves as a blotter page to absorb marker ink that might bleed through while coloring.

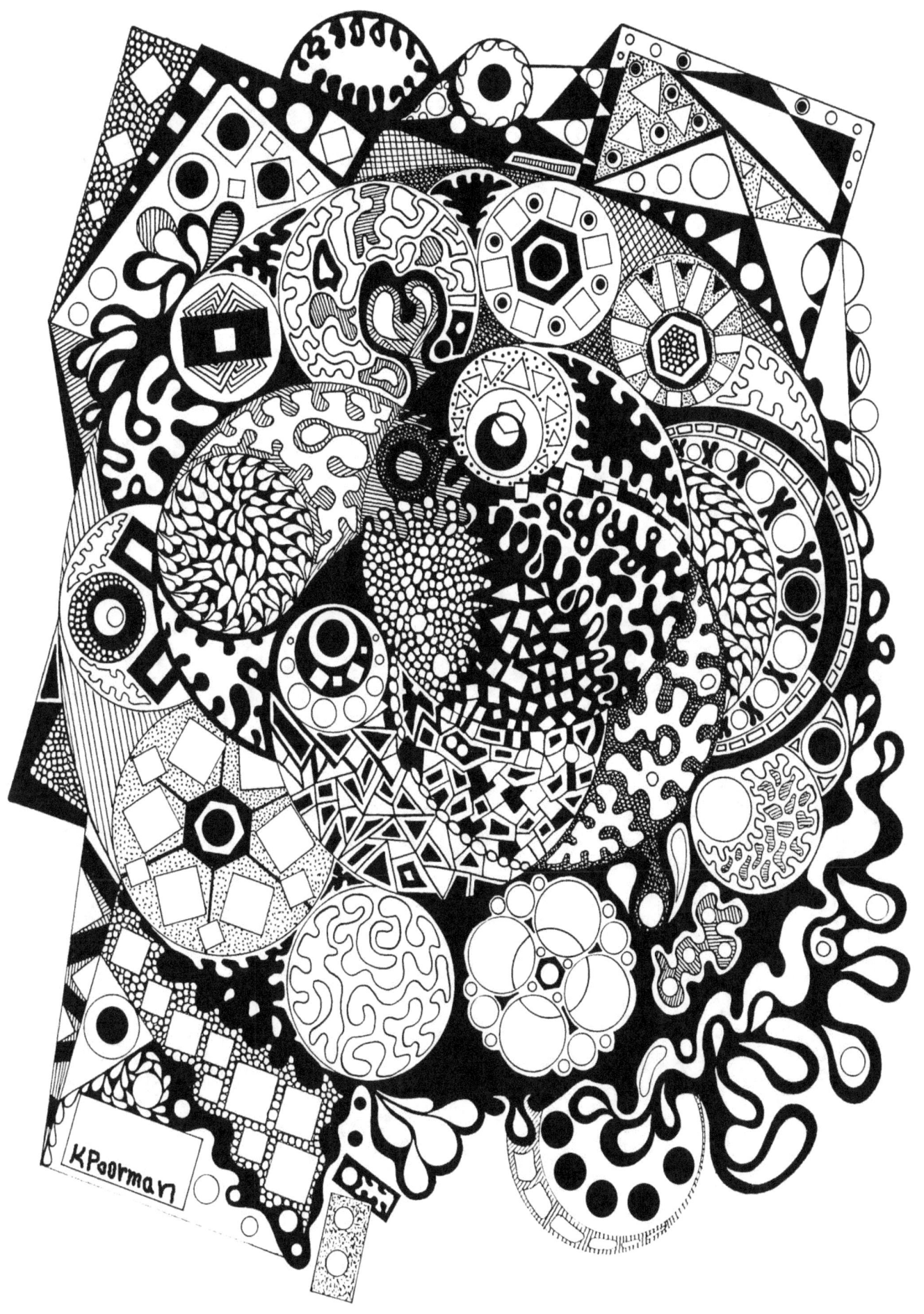

This blank page serves as a
blotter page to absorb marker
ink that might bleed through
while coloring.

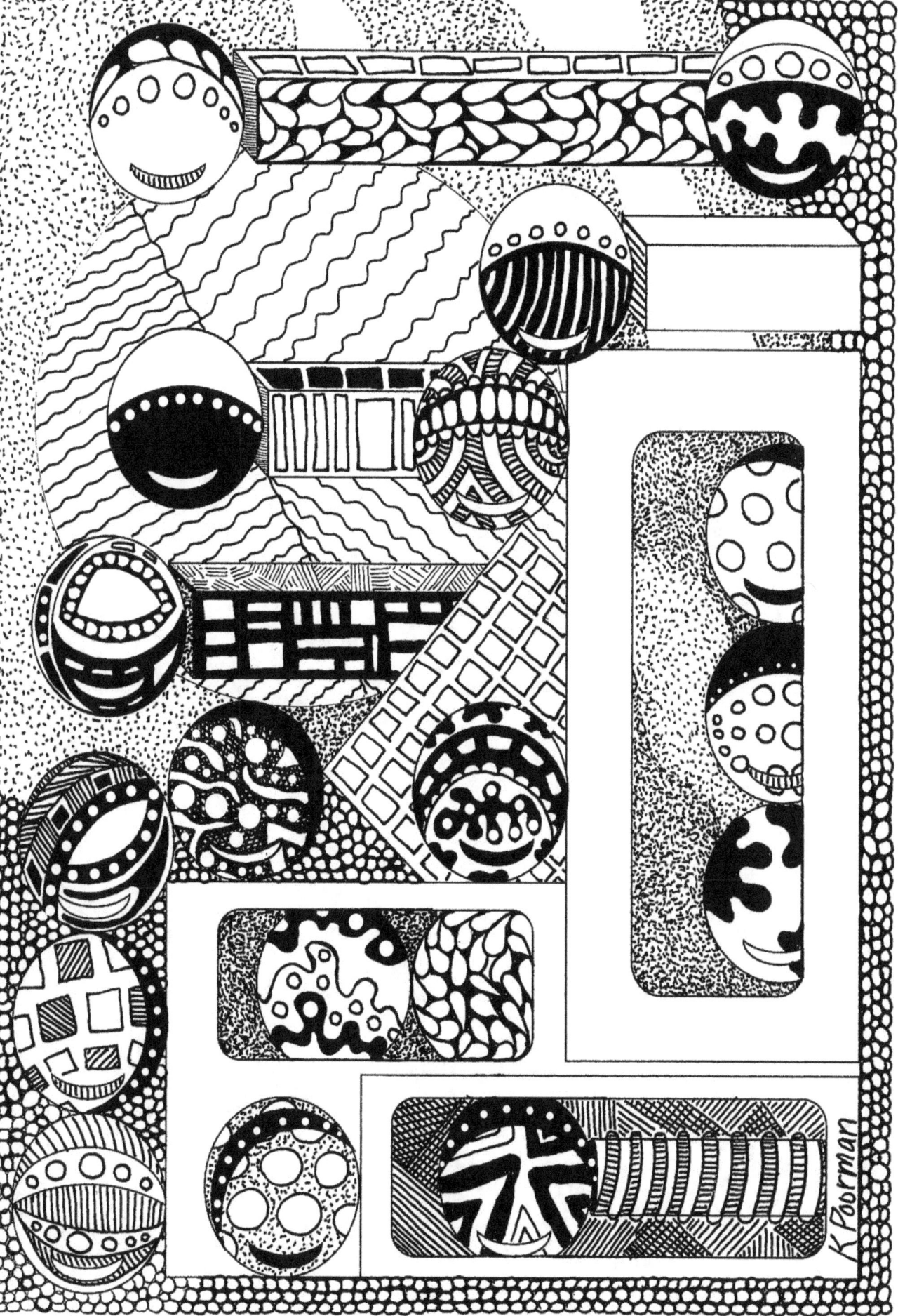

This blank page serves as a blotter page to absorb marker ink that might bleed through while coloring.

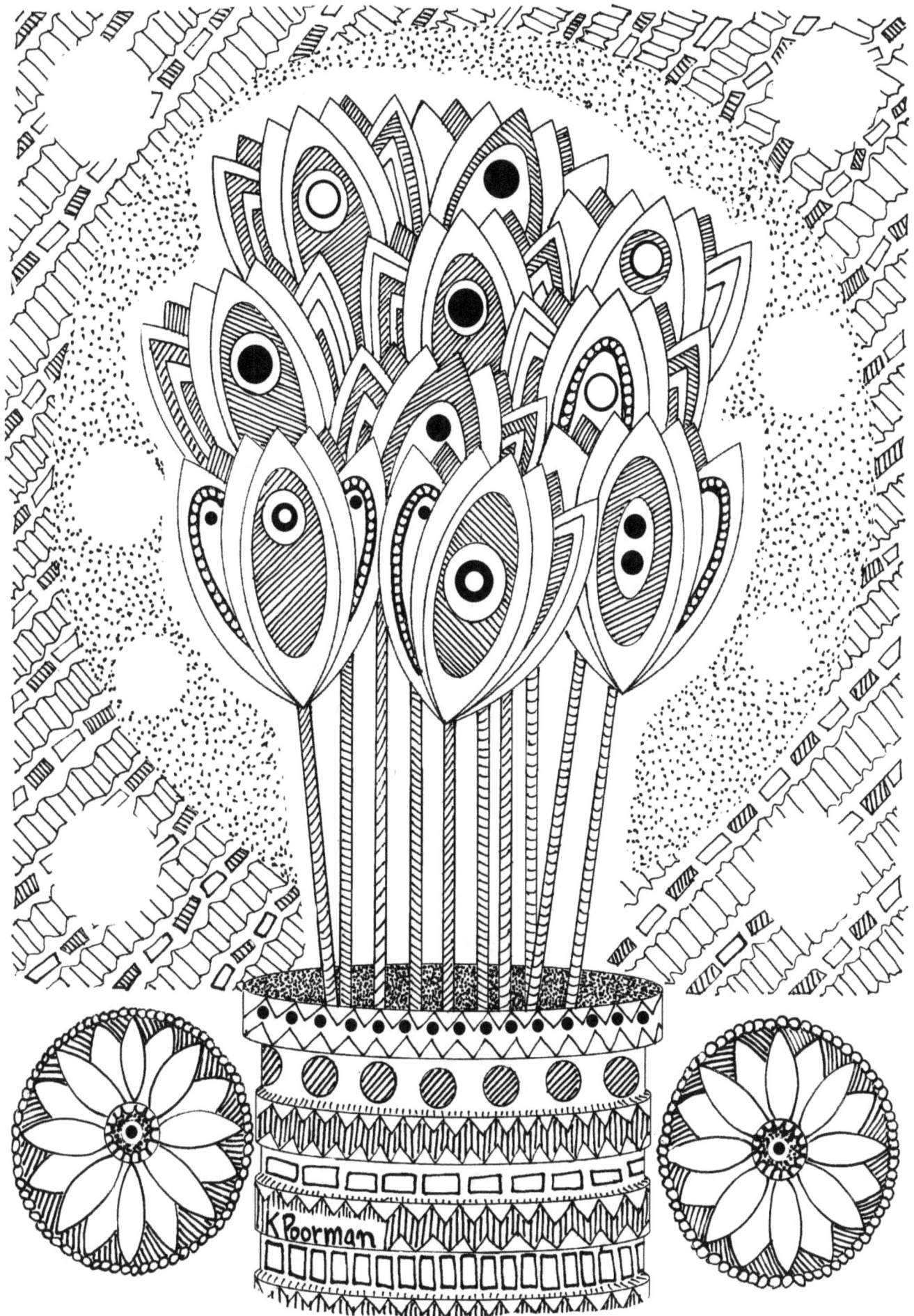

This blank page serves as a
blotter page to absorb marker
ink that might bleed through
while coloring.

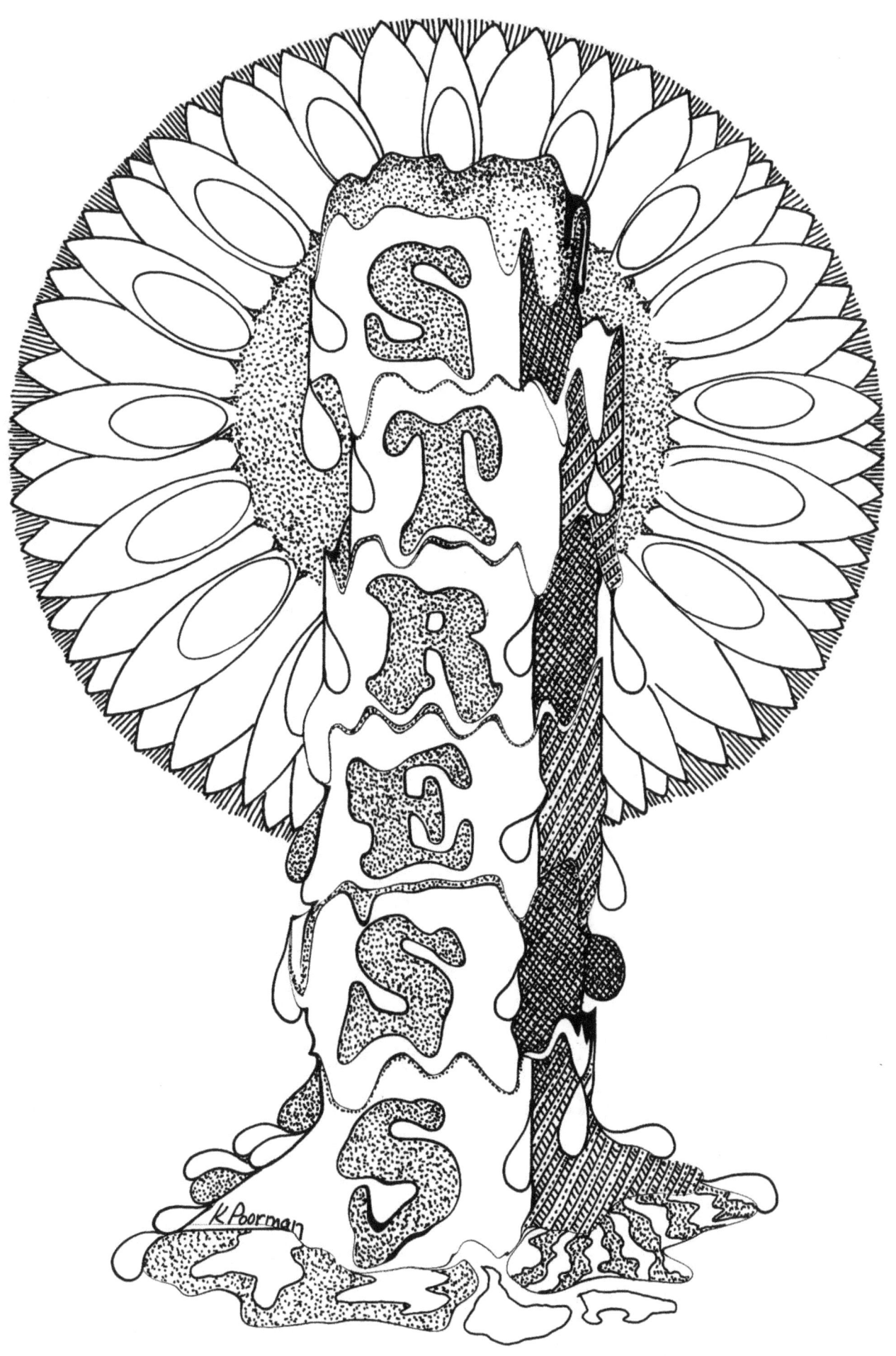

This blank page serves as a
blotter page to absorb marker
ink that might bleed through
while coloring.

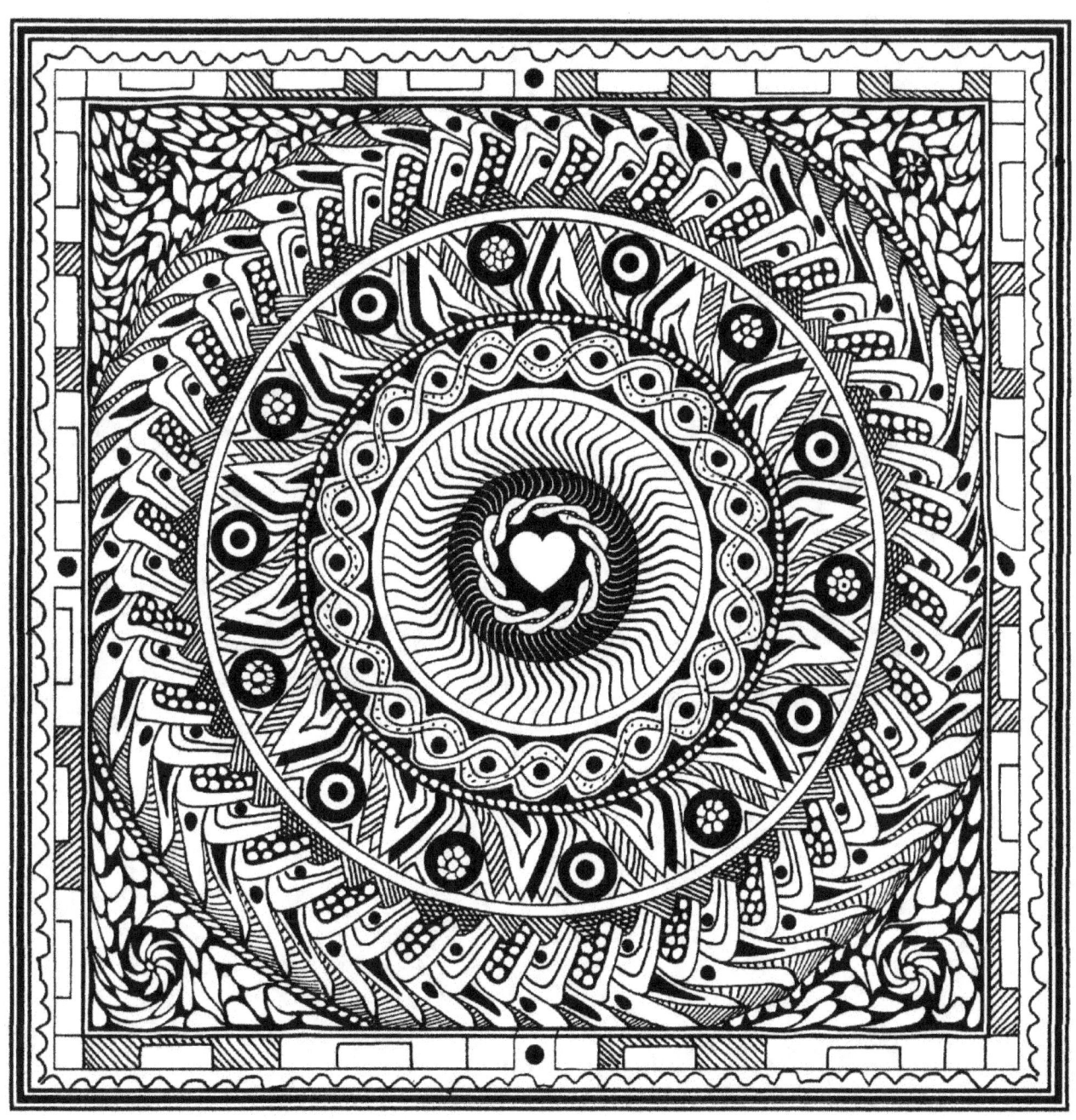

Home Is Where The Heart Is

This blank page serves as a
blotter page to absorb marker
ink that might bleed through
while coloring.

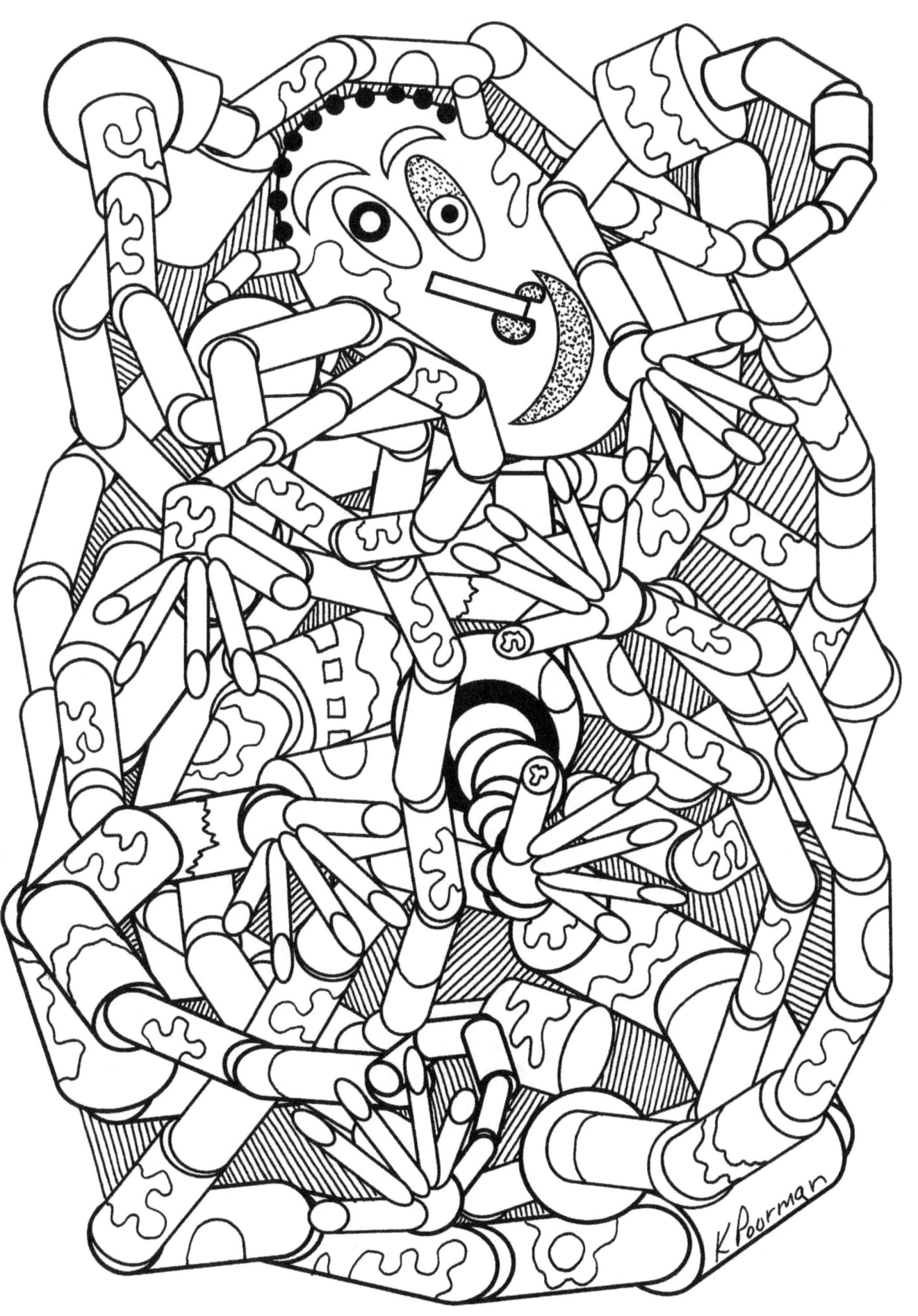

This blank page serves as a blotter page to absorb marker ink that might bleed through while coloring.

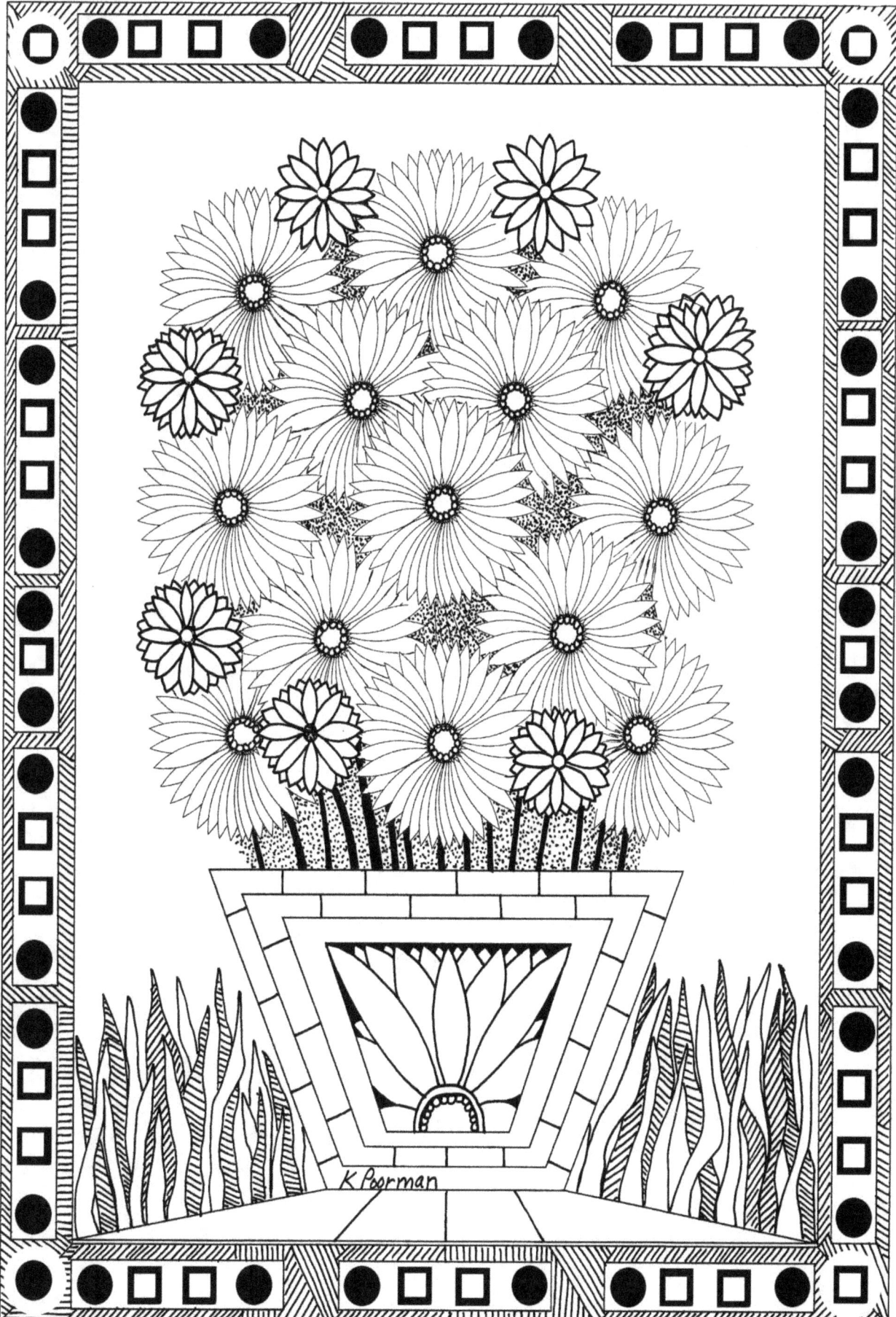

This blank page serves as a
blotter page to absorb marker
ink that might bleed through
while coloring.

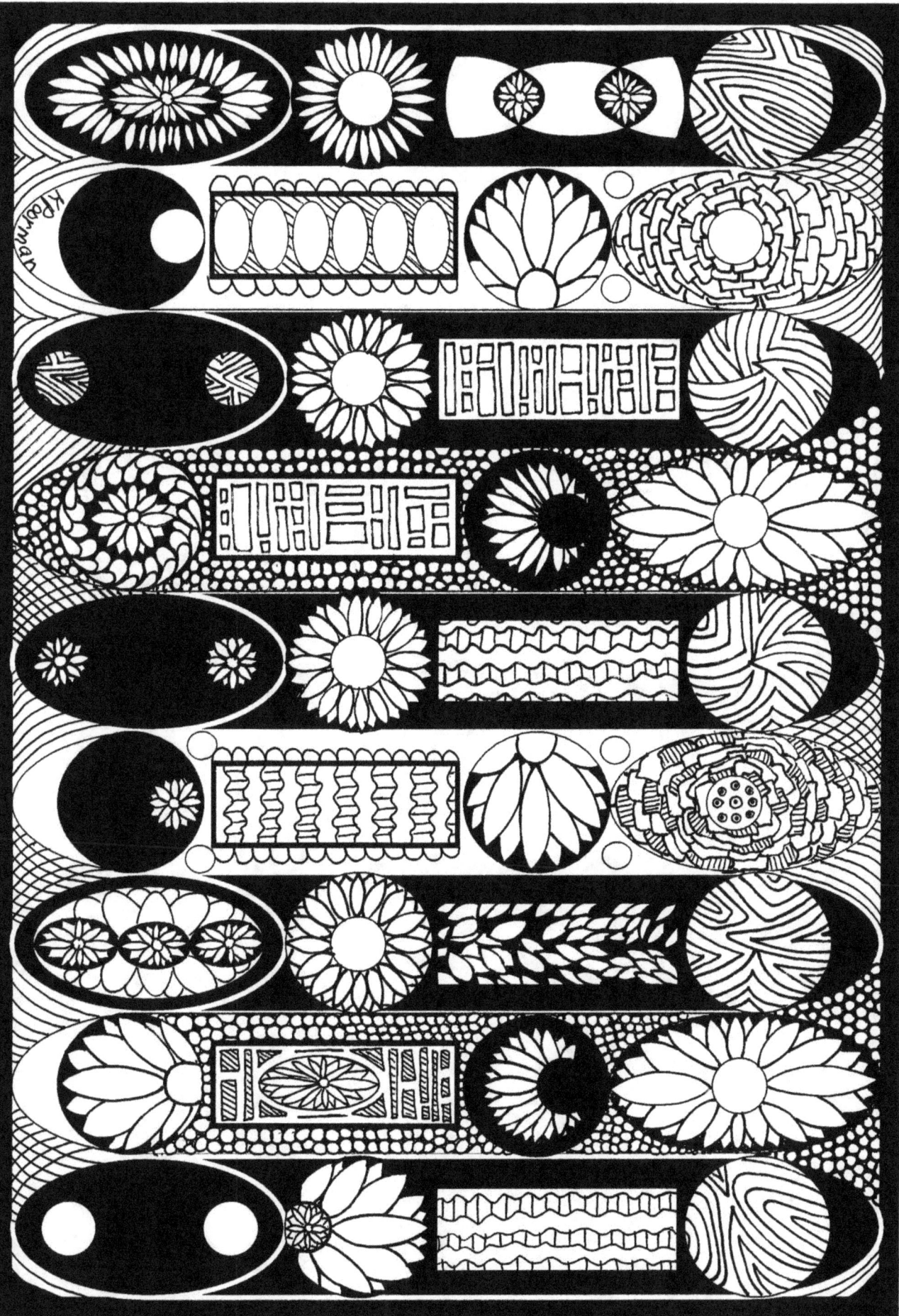

This blank page serves as a
blotter page to absorb marker
ink that might bleed through
while coloring.

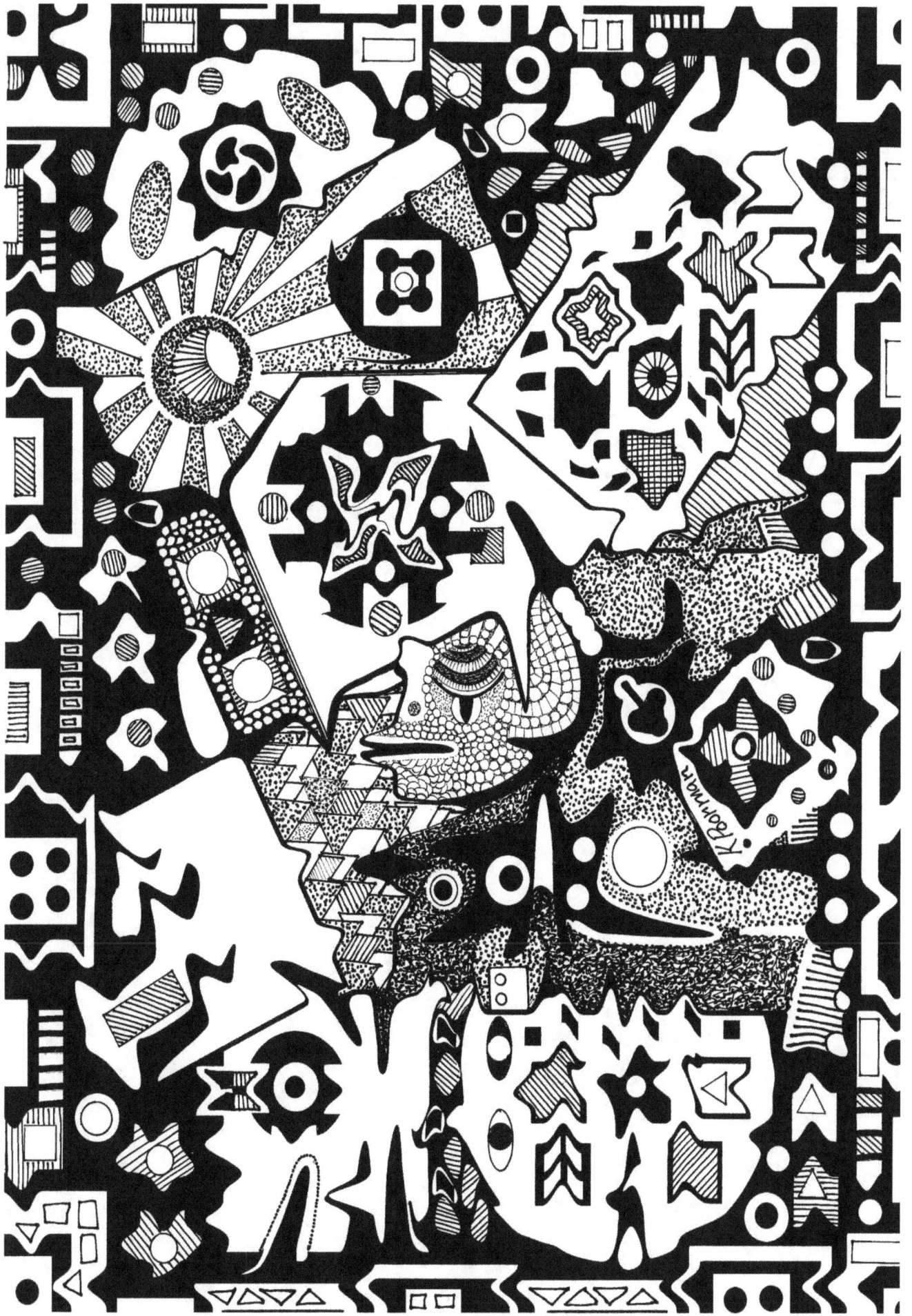

This blank page serves as a blotter page to absorb marker ink that might bleed through while coloring.